D1438938

Exploring British Values

Obeying the Law

Catherine Chambers

a Capstone company — publishers for children

Raintree is an imprint of Capstone Global Library Limited, a company incorporated in England and Wales having its registered office at 264 Banbury Road, Oxford, OX2 7DY – Registered company number: 6695582

www.raintree.co.uk
myorders@raintree.co.uk

Text © Capstone Global Library Limited 2018

Edited by Linda Staniford
Designed by Terri Poburka
Picture research by Pam Mitsakos
Original illustrations © Capstone Global Library Limited 2018
Illustrated by Graham Ross
Production by Steve Walker
Originated by Capstone Global Library
Printed and bound in China

ISBN 978 1 474 74078 4
21 20 19 18 17
10 9 8 7 6 5 4 3 2 1

British Library Cataloguing in Publication Data
A full catalogue record for this book is available from the British Library.

Acknowledgements
We would like to thank the following for permission to reproduce photographs: Alamy: format4, 5, James Brunker UK, 13, Peter Titmuss, 17, REUTERS, 27, richard mittleman, 11; Getty Images: Andrew Aitchison/Pictures Ltd./Corbis, 24-25; iStockphoto: michael_price, cover bottom, traveler1116, 7; Newscom: PEAA/ZDS/WENN, 19; Shutterstock: 1000 Words, 21, Attitude, design element, Ermine, design element, Lifestyle_Studio, design element, olavs, 8-9, Sarunyu_foto, design element, Twin Design, 28-29, URRRA, design element; The Image Works: © iD8/John Birdsall, 23; Thinkstock: Baloncici, 15

We would like to thank Marguerite Heath, Programmes Director at the Citizenship Foundation, for her invaluable help in the preparation of this book.

Contents

Some words are shown in bold, **like this**. You can find out what they mean by looking in the glossary.

What is meant by obeying the law?

Obeying the law is one of four key British values. These values help people to understand how to behave.

Obeying the law means following rules that protect us all from harm. In Britain, government makes and passes laws that bring peace, safety and community harmony. When people break the law, they cause hurt and **conflict** in our society.

Britain is made up of four separate countries: England, Northern Ireland, Scotland and Wales. Each country has slightly different laws, but their aims and values are the same.

Rules in our lives

There are many rules in our lives. They are not always laws that are made by Parliament. But they guide us when we play a sport or join a club, or when we go to school or work. There are also codes of **behaviour**, which are about how we treat each other.

The Task Team investigates

Amina, Emily and Kwame are the Task Team. They report on school and community issues for their class. This time, the team investigates obeying the law through a local incident.

4

We obey laws every day. This London bus has to stop at temporary traffic lights.

British values are about treating everyone equally. We are all equal in law, whatever our gender, age, ethnic background, birthplace or faith. That means our laws are the same for all of us. This encourages us to treat each other the same in our daily lives.

Fact FILE

Laws include:

- **Byelaws.** These are local laws such as riding on pavements, behaviour on our streets and car parking.

- **Criminal laws.** These are national laws about crimes such as violence and theft.

- **Civil laws.** These are laws that allow a person to take someone to court, for example, when someone is cheated out of money.

Where did our laws come from?

British laws are national laws that are followed by citizens of England, Wales, Scotland and Northern Ireland. Everyone has to obey these laws. But it took a long time before people in power had to obey them.

Our laws were shaped over a period of at least 2,000 years. For a long time, they were based on ancient Roman law. Then, Christian **Catholic** Church law took over and lasted for hundreds of years.

Leaders and laws

In Medieval times (1066–1485), kings and queens of Britain's kingdoms collected taxes and led armies. But they did not make laws for their people. Laws were made by the leaders of the Catholic Church in Rome. Catholic priests judged and punished people who broke the laws.

Church law changes to state laws

About 800 years ago, King Henry II (1133–1189) of England sent his own judges to sort out crimes across the land. But the Catholic priests were not allowed to take part in the judges' trials. From this point, English state law, or national law, began to separate from Church law.

Medieval kings and queens were able to disobey the law. Then in 1215, barons forced King John I (1167–1216) to sign a document called the Magna Carta. From this time, kings and queens had to obey the law.

Barons were angry that King John used his powers to tax them heavily.

It's against the law to damage my goods with a scooter!

Yes, but it's too dangerous for kids to scoot in the road.

Maybe we can talk about it at school?

Yes. We should set some rules.

English state law developed over the next 800 years, but there were problems along the way. Sometimes, rulers did not obey the nation's laws. Or they decided that some people should be treated worse than others. Today, the law says all people should be treated the same. The idea of **equality** is a British value.

Making law and making judgement

The British government designs laws and Parliament passes laws. But they are not allowed to judge anyone accused of breaking those laws. This is the job of the **judiciary**, which is our court system.

It is important to separate government from the judiciary. Government cannot judge itself or use its power to ignore laws and escape justice. If it did do that, it could be accused of breaking the law.

Laws in all four countries

Parliament passes many laws for the whole of Britain. But the Scottish Parliament, Welsh Assembly and Northern Ireland Assembly also pass laws that directly affect their own people. These separate powers are known as devolved powers, or **devolution**. They were granted by Parliament in 1999.

Laws are made in the Houses of Parliament on London's River Thames.

Fact FILE

Ancient Christian laws are still the basis of many British laws. But for hundreds of years people of other faiths have lived in Britain. Everyone must obey British law. However, some family issues can be resolved in religious courts under systems of law such as these:

- Halakha law, followed in Judaism.
- Sharia law, followed in Islam.

How we behave

There are hundreds of laws in Britain and new ones are made all the time. These are written rules. But there are other rules that are not written down. These are the rules of **behaviour** and manners. They are about being kind, helpful, welcoming and respectful to people around us.

Making rules

Most of us try to treat each other with **respect**. This is because we think about other people and care about their feelings. It is hard to know what to do when others in a group behave differently.

We can ask others why they are behaving in a disrespectful way and discuss it. We can decide whether the group is being fair or if it excludes some people. We might have to change the rules to allow for differences. The people who behaved differently might have to learn to fit in better, too. This process is how rules and laws are changed, wherever we are.

School rules

At school, rules create a calm **atmosphere** to learn in. Sometimes rules need to be discussed and changed to make them fairer. At other times they need to keep pace with modern life and new technology, just like state laws.

From reading the Highway Code, I reckon that scooting on pavements is PROBABLY not allowed. Hmmm.

There MUST be a solution.

Of course! Scooting's like cycling. It's all about the wheels!

YOU Decide!

Get together with others and discuss the fairness of school rules. Could any be changed to make them fairer? If so, take your ideas to your class teacher or school council.

CLASS RULES

1. Listen when others are talking.

2. Follow directions.

3. Keep hands, feet, and objects to yourself.

4. Work quietly and do not disturb others.

5. Show respect for school and personal property.

6. Work and play in a safe manner.

© Carson-Dellosa CD-6265

Printed in the USA

Listening tops these class rules. Listening allows us to gather opinions and facts.

11

The laws around us

There are many local laws that affect us in the area where we live. They are called **byelaws**. Byelaws are made by our local councils.

Local council decisions aim to help organisations and services run smoothly. These include schools, hospitals, police stations, community centres and sports venues. Councils try to make sure that our streets are clean and peaceful, too.

Different places; different byelaws

Villages, towns and cities each have different needs and problems. This means that their local councils make different byelaws.

In cities, there may be special byelaws for riding bikes in cycle lanes. In the countryside, byelaws might stop off-road biking in fields. On the coast, local laws against dogs fouling on beaches could be in force. So when we travel, it is important to understand each local environment and the people who live there. Then we can respect their needs and rules.

What brings us together?

Some issues are the same for all of us, wherever we live. One of these is caring for the environment. It includes not dropping litter and making sure we recycle our rubbish. These are things that show we respect the place where we live. They are not always enforced by law.

Get INVOLVED!

Can you think of a project that would improve your local environment? It might be organising a clean-up of a wildlife area, for example. You could put together a report and present it to your local **councillor**.

These byelaws help people stay safe in the sea and keep beaches clean.

No Fouling

Clean It Up
Please clean up after your dog
Maximum Penalty £1000

Dogs allowed

⚠ CAUTION ⚠
BEACH LEVELS MAY CHANGE
FOR YOUR SAFETY KEEP OFF GROYNES AND OTHER STRUCTURES

HASTINGS BOROUGH COUNCIL
BYELAWS
NAVIGATION OF SAILBOARDS

The above Byelaws make it an offence punishable by a maximum fine of £100 for a person to cause or permit a sailboard to be sailed or otherwise propelled to the danger of bathers on any part of the Foreshore.

Hmm. It tells us about RESPONSIBLE scooting and cycling for kids.

But what does responsible scooting MEAN? How can we make rules?

13

Keeping us safe

Many national laws and local byelaws help to keep us safe. They are also made to keep us from harming others. These laws include respecting the rights of others when we ride our scooters or bikes, or when we play ball games in a public place such as a park.

Sometimes we have to follow safety rules that are not local or national laws. Bus and train companies have these kinds of rules to protect us when we travel. So do managers of buildings such as shops and museums.

Making standards

Laws, or **regulations**, also ensure our food is safe to eat and our water clean enough to drink. The toys you play with and the equipment you use are all made according to safety laws. These are based on safety standards that are recommended by scientists and engineers.

Standards change with time as science and technology improve materials and ways of manufacturing the things we buy. At the same time, safety laws that enforce those standards change, too. New standards and new products require new safety laws. So making these laws is a continuous process.

Get INVOLVED!

Find out about special byelaws in your area. Why have they been made? Make a slogan, poem or poster pointing out why a byelaw needs to be followed in your area.

Food standards and faith

Our food is farmed, processed and sold according to safety laws. People of different faiths follow other food laws, too. For example, in Islam and Judaism, food should be chosen and prepared according to laws in these faiths' holy books, the Qu'ran and Torah. These are not local or national laws. But they are very important to followers of different faiths.

These regulations are clearly displayed to keep people safe on a building site.

Who makes laws?

British laws are made in Parliament. **Members of Parliament**, or MPs, vote for or against a new law or a change in an old law.

Choosing the lawmakers

In Britain, adults over the age of 18 can vote for an MP for the area in which they live. The freedom to vote for, or elect, MPs is called **democracy**, which is another important British value.

Voters elect the person they think will pass the best laws in Parliament. They hope that the person will make good changes in their area, too. Voters can also elect local **councillors**. These are the people who make decisions on our local councils.

Fact FILE

A **petition** is a written protest to government on a law or issue. A petition needs:

- 10,000 signatures to get a reply from government.
- 100,000 signatures to get a debate in Parliament.

Two voters mark their ballot papers in a polling booth on election day.

Listening to ideas

Most elected MPs and local councillors belong to political parties. These are organisations whose members share similar ideas. It is important to listen to their ideas so that we can vote wisely.

Giving ideas – making changes

We can get involved in changing and making laws. This is called lobbying. We can present our ideas to our local MP in a letter, email or survey. We can also invite our MP to a meeting or event. Another way to get involved is to start a **petition**. This is a written request to the government about an issue or cause. It's usually signed by a lot of people who all feel strongly about the issue.

How are broken laws policed?

We all do things that are wrong sometimes. However, most people do not break a law on purpose. When laws are broken, a crime has been committed. Some crimes are more serious than others, but they all affect people, their property or the environment. Crimes are policed in different ways.

Policing the streets

You might see police community support officers (PCSOs) on the streets where you live. The PCSO's role is to ask questions about local crimes and give information to the regular police. They chat to people, asking if there are any problems in the area. They might also give people warnings or advice. For example, an officer may point out to a child that they are cycling dangerously, or warn someone against writing graffiti on a wall.

Tackling serious crime

Regular police officers patrol the streets giving warnings and advice, too. They are also involved in solving serious crimes. They give information to senior officers and the National Crime Agency. Crimes organised on the internet are investigated by the National Cyber Crime Agency.

Serious crimes include murder and armed robbery. They often involve **criminal** gangs. These gangs might be involved in people **trafficking**. This is when people from other countries are forced to work in terrible conditions in another country, such as Britain.

When someone is suspected of a crime, what happens next?

Get INVOLVED!

See if you can conduct a survey in school to see which types of antisocial **behaviour** affect your community most. Then create a short play with others to show how antisocial behaviour affects people.

In London, police keep Victoria railway station safe and help lost travellers too.

19

Gathering the facts

Gathering facts, or **evidence**, is an important part of police work. Police investigators try to match the evidence to their suspect – the person they think committed the crime.

If the evidence shows clearly that the suspect is guilty, then the police might charge the suspect with the crime. They might give the suspect a caution, or warning. Or the suspect may be sent for trial in a court of law. This is the first stage of our judicial system.

In British law, a person is seen as innocent unless the facts prove them to be guilty. There are three main courts in Britain.

Magistrates' courts

All suspects are sent to a **magistrates'** court first. If the crime is very serious, the court sends the suspect to a higher court for trial. This is called the Crown court.

A magistrates' court can judge less serious crimes. These include minor damage to property, some driving offences, theft, small-scale burglary, disturbing people too much or being involved with bad drugs. Magistrates' courts are also in charge of youth courts.

Youth courts

Youth courts judge children up to 17 years of age. The crimes they judge include theft, burglary, antisocial **behaviour**, such as violence or damage, and drug offences.

Crown courts

Crown courts judge suspects accused of very serious offences. These include murder, violent attacks on people and property, and serious robbery.

Higher justice

Sometimes victims or those accused of crime do not agree with the **verdict** of a court. So they make an appeal. This means they take their case to a higher court, hoping for a different verdict. The highest of all is the Supreme Court, which was opened in 2009.

Some local councils give spaces for graffiti artists to work legally.

Get INVOLVED!

Can you see damage, graffiti and rubbish that spoil your area? With others, you could record the problem in writing, with pictures and a map. Then ask your local council to help create a clean-up plan.

I'm giving you a warning, Archie! And I'm telling the school.

I bet we won't be able to scoot AT ALL now. Thanks A LOT, Archie!

What happens in court?

In court, the police need to put forward their argument, or case, against the suspect. This is called the case for the **prosecution**. Legal experts advise the police in court.

The suspect also needs to put forward his or her case. This is called the case for the **defence**. A legal expert called a **solicitor** represents the suspect in court.

In a magistrates' court

Two or three magistrates or a district judge are in charge of the Magistrates' Court. Sometimes the suspect is found innocent. But if someone is found guilty, a magistrate can sentence the person. The punishment will depend on the crime the suspect committed. It might be detention, or prison, for six months. It might be working on a Community Service project. Community Service is unpaid work that benefits the community, such as removing graffiti. Or it could be a fine of up to £5,000.

In a youth court

Three magistrates or a district judge sit on the Youth Court. A young person who is found guilty might be asked to apologise to their victim or to mend any damage. Offenders might be sent to classes that make them understand the harm they caused. Some may be fined, or sent to Community Service or a **detention centre**.

In a Crown Court

The Crown Court is led by a judge. Twelve British citizens, called the **jury**, are chosen to listen to the evidence. They listen to **witnesses** who tell what they saw or heard about the crime. From all this, the jury decides if a person is innocent or guilty. The judge then sentences the person to pay a fine, to Community Service or to prison.

A judge can advise or direct a jury, but the can reject the direction.

YOU Decide!

Prisoners are not allowed to vote, so they have no involvement in politics and law making. Do you think this is fair or helpful?

So what do YOU say. Archie?

I'm really sorry. I let us all down.

Thank you. Archie. The head teacher and I will discuss it.

Does our justice system work?

People are judged on the facts presented in court. But sometimes mistakes are made in gathering the facts. Sometimes evidence may be missing or recorded wrongly. A witness might give poor evidence. This means that someone might be found guilty or innocent by mistake.

Treating people equally

Our system of judging people fairly depends on the magistrates, judges and jury members looking at the facts. They must try not to judge a person for any other reason. They must not judge a suspect unfairly because of the suspect's ethnic background, colour, faith, or whether he or she is rich or poor. If they do, this is called **prejudice** and it can lead to mistakes in our judicial system.

Do our punishments work?

Magistrates and judges have to think about victims of crime. If victims have been badly harmed, a judge might send the accused person to prison for a long time. Judges hope that this will stop other people from behaving in the same way.

But prison does not work for a lot of people. Many commit crimes again after they have been released. This is called reoffending. Reoffending happens much less when prisoners are given education and training. For example, some prisoners have been trained to set up successful restaurants inside the prison grounds.

Between 2014 and 2015, over 24 per cent of adults sent to prison reoffended after they had been released. Nearly 38 per cent of young people reoffended.

In law, a prisoner has the right to be in the open air for 30 to 60 minutes every day.

Yes. He's restless ALL the time. He can't control his movements.

And he can't help it. So it would be a shame to stop him scooting.

Hmmm. I see. But we shopkeepers have a problem too!

Laws around the world – and us

Sometimes we have different rules of **behaviour** from our friends, and this can cause problems. It is important that the whole group shares the same basic values. This is the same for Britain's laws and values, which we may not share with all countries.

International laws and values

International organisations such as the **United Nations (UN)** set out laws and values that countries can aim to abide by. The United Nations was set up in 1945. It was created to keep world peace after World War II (1939-1945) and now has 193 member states.

The UN's laws are based on its Universal Declaration of Human Rights, created in 1948. This is a list of 30 rights and freedoms that all people should enjoy, such as the right to life, **liberty** and security. Many British laws include these values, too.

YOU Decide!

Is it right to trade, visit and talk with a nation that breaks UN laws? If we do, we are helping them. If we do not, then we cannot encourage them to change their policies.

What do you think the problem is?

Well. I think scooter LAWS for kids should be clearer.

What happens when we do not share laws

Some UN member countries break UN laws. They make war on other countries or on their own people. They use terrible weapons that are against UN laws.

Even so, countries outside the **conflict** still trade and talk with these countries. This means that they are breaking UN **regulations**. The UN members then meet together. They try to find ways of making a warring country and its allies return to shared laws.

The UN's peacekeeping forces are gathered from its member countries.

Maybe we can use ideas from other countries?

Mmm. Good idea!

Like in New South Wales, Australia. They put up signs for scooters, skateboards and rollerblades in danger zones.

The future for British values in law

Law and order help us to keep British values. British values are a stable foundation on which to make laws. This important link between law and values will help us as Britain changes. It will help us as the world around us changes, too. We will be able to make new laws that are fair, kind and respect **equality**.

We must take responsibility

Parliament and our local councils cannot make laws and uphold values on their own. We can all help. We can listen to the needs of people around us and consider whether our laws help them. We can find reliable news stories and facts to help us develop our own ideas.

Keeping up with crime

The internet is a wonderful way of finding out about the world and connecting with people. But some people use new technology to commit crime. Britain's police and information-gathering organisations work hard to keep up with this.

Sometimes adults use the internet, especially social media, to make young people do things that they do not want to do. At other times adults use the internet to steal from people.

Keeping safe

It is important to keep up with the latest ways of protecting ourselves and the people around us. There are plenty of security apps that can help keep us safe.

It is also important that we treat each other kindly when we use new digital media. This is an unwritten law that helps each one of us, and our communities.

Get INVOLVED!

With the help of responsible adults, learn as much as you can about keeping safe online. Learn about the laws that can be broken online and how not to break them yourself. Then you can help others who do not know them.

If you know about online protection, you can share your knowledge with friends.

29

Glossary

atmosphere feeling or mood in a place

behaviour the way a person acts

byelaw rule made by a local council for the regulation of its affairs or management of the area it governs

Catholic relating to the Roman Catholic church; the religion followed in Britain until the 16th century

civil relating to citizens as individuals

conflict disagreement

councillor member of a local council who makes decisions at a local level

criminal involving crime

defence legal proceedings in support of a person suspected of committing a crime

democracy type of government in which the people elect their leaders

a place where people awaiting trial may stay for a short time by order of a court

devolution transfer of authority from a central government to regional governments; the powers transferred are called devolved powers

equality the same rights for everyone

evidence information produced in a court of law to support a case, such as the statements of witnesses, documents and material objects

judiciary system of courts of justice in a country

jury a group of, usually twelve, people sworn to deliver a true verdict on a case based on the evidence presented in a court of law

liberty freedom from restriction or control

magistrate public officer concerned with the administration of law

Member of Parliament (MP) person elected by people living in a particular area to represent them in the House of Commons

petition document signed by a large number of people demanding action from a government or other authority

prejudice hatred or unfair treatment of people who belong to a certain social group, such as an ethnic background or religion

prosecution legal proceedings against person accused of committing a crime

regulation rule that governs procedure or behaviour

respect accept a person as a human being and that they have rights

solicitor a lawyer who advises clients on matters of law and may represent clients in court

trafficking trade in human beings for the purpose of exploitation

verdict jury's answer given to a court concerning a matter they have been asked to judge

United Nations (UN) international organization formed to keep peace in the world and to defend human rights

witness person who has seen or can give first-hand evidence of an event

Find out more

Books

You might like to look at these other books on British Values:

It's the Law! (British Values), Christopher Yeates (Gresham Books, 2016)

Let's Vote on it! (British Values), Christopher Yeates (Gresham Books, 2016)

Looking After Britain (British Values), Christopher Yeates (Gresham Books, 2016)

What Does It Mean to be British?, Nick Hunter (Raintree, 2017)

Websites

www.bbc.co.uk/newsround
The CBBC Newsround website gives lots of interesting features on rights and values around the world.

www.parliament.uk/documents/education/online-resources/printed-resources/Parliament-laws-and-you-ks2-illustrated-booklet.pdf
On this site you can find out more about how laws are made in Parliament.

www.un.org/en/universal-declaration-human-rights/
On this site you can read the United Nations Declaration of Human Rights.

Index